Discovering
GOD'S
Heart

More Books in the Series:

Discovering God's Sufficiency
Going beyond ourselves and experiencing the supernatural
Pastoral Health Care — Part One

Discovering God's Love
Confirming God's love through the evidence of historical facts
Pastoral Health Care — Part Two

Discovering God's Counsel
Applying his spiritual solution to meet difficult trials
Pastoral Health Care — Part Three

Discovering God's Kingdom
Finding a way to understand ourselves in a complex world
Pastoral Health Care — Part Four

"I have ALS which means that my life is being taken away from me. Don't ask me how I am doing. Every day brings new challenges but I am learning to live each moment with God's presence. I am comforted knowing that the Holy Spirit is traveling each step with me. I ask for his filling every day and even every hour. I am assured of my future with Jesus. As I meditate on his Word, he provides me with his perspective on life — death and all the stuff in between. I will reach my destiny with my team supporters."

— Cindy Smith

"I am 100 years old and have all the special physical needs that people my age experience. The spiritual Biblical mediation method works for me. It has strengthened my faith. As I recite the promises, they become a part of my thinking process. My fellowship with God provides natural growth for me both internally and externally. I am thankful that I live with His presence."

— William Mulder

"I have grown up with seizures. I know what it is like to lose consciousness. I know my illness is a brain disorder that requires prescribed medicines regularly. Adjusting to the various dosages is a pain. I hate the side effects that I live with. I am enabled through the guidance of the Bible. It keeps reminding me of 'His' nearness. I am thankful for the support I have. I miss my former life and its activities. My prayer is always "keep me close to you, God, and my family!" Discovering God's Sufficiency has challenged me to be close to Jesus Christ."

— George Odiorne

"My Life has always looked a little different. I was born with spina bifida and fluid on my brain. I have to live with many side effects like sore back, loss of balance, terrible headaches and short term memory. I have been able to manage every day remembering that God has a purpose for my life. I have been blessed with a family that I need to be here for. Every day brings new challenges that have turned my spirit toward Scripture. To my amazement, God has promised to help me. I can't count the times that I have felt His presence. I know that God has a plan for me and he will accomplish it according to his will."

— *Judy Sharp*

"I have had MS for several years. At the present time, I have been experiencing intense nerve pain. My relationship with Christ has helped me make the adjustments that are needed to survive. I am comforted to know that I will not be stretched beyond my ability to bear. I have confidence that God's will will be accomplished in my life. I have my destiny in heaven where I will experience perfection. I know abiding in Christ is the key."

— *Chuck Boomgard*

"I live with Multiple Sclerosis which is a neurological disease that affects every part of my body. I never know from one day to the next how my body is going to be. I have more MS days than functional days. While losing my worldly independence, I have gained a powerful relationship with my God by choosing to depend upon him. My trust in God empowers me to face every day with joy."

— *Susan Clark Denny*

John Gillette's writings flow from a lifetime of experience. It is one thing to write out of a knowledge based on research. It is an entirely different thing to write out of a depth of life experience. John has both. As a pastor who has cared for the needs of a congregation, as a husband who has experienced the tragic loss of a wife, and as a child of God who has walked through the joys and pain of following the Lord, John has so much to offer in this series. From the opening pages, through to the very end, you will be blessed by the insights, loving tone and encouragement you receive from this series. God has used John greatly in ministry and will continue to use him through this life-giving series.

—*Josh Mateer, D. Min.*

True, illustrative, practical stories are like windows that unlock Bible truths and promises. Along with a masterfully orchestrated short stories should come the truth that God's Word and love has been experienced by His servants as they partner with Him in the work of rebuilding the Kingdom. A gifted teacher, Dr. Gillette lives an ordinary life abiding in Christ and being an obedient servant of the Lord. As he sees God working in his life, and in the lives of those to whom he ministers, his faith is refreshed and he is encouraged to press on through life's uncertainties.

Only a lifetime dedicated to nurturing, ministering, teaching, and keen insight through the power of the Holy Spirit, can produce such poignant stories that teach and challenge.

—*Mulonge M. Kalumbula, Ph.D.*

John's books give us hope and light. He reminds us that through Jesus we are never alone. I have certainly needed that reminder in my life and in my practice. In holding a patient's hand, and helping them through a condition or disease, reminding them that they are never alone has become the greatest gift of health care.

—*Linda M. Kunce, D.C.*

The series reminds me that Jesus knows what it's like to live in a human body. I have received Jesus and His forgiveness, but as the book suggests, I also have the power from the Holy Spirit. His books have encouraged me to gain courage through prayer and confidence in Jesus to meet my needs. John's honesty is very special to read as he reflects on his own life and struggles. I like his explanation that "the soul is where the emotions are and the mind is where the thinking takes place". It's been good for me to read that God works through weakness, and learn that John found God with him in the middle of the struggles.

—*Arvid W. Vandyke, Ed.D.*

Discovering God's Counsel is a book full of great spiritual truths from someone who has developed a very close and deep relationship with Jesus through his life. John provides a meaningful and inspirational testimony, with examples from his own experiences, of how relying on God's Word and promises can give you the power, hope, and peace you need to overcome life's struggles and challenges. The Scriptures he chose in his book were on point and helpful. It was an enjoyable and wonderful read.

—*Thoa Reyna, J.D.*

John has written a user-friendly and practical series for anyone desiring to live beyond the superficial and venture into the supernatural. The world needs this *Pastoral Health Care Series*. Pastors and followers of Jesus need the insights from John's lifetime experience of walking with God and caring for His people through the power of the Holy Spirit. John has brilliantly show that God is enough, God's love is real, God's counsel is enduring, and God reigns supremely. This important series will serve both the church and the world for many years to come.

—*Kizombo Kalumbula, Jr., Ph.D.*

Note from the Author

I believe in God's sovereignty and compassion. I am learning to let go of self and to hold onto someone that can do whatever he pleases. Sometimes life is cruel, sometimes it is full of suffering, physically and psychological. A spiritual solution to meet difficult trials has become my goal. God's word carries with it no uncertainties. I want it to saturate my mind and heart.

The *Pastoral Health Care Series* was created through unexpected heart disease (open heart surgery), cancer (medication and surgery), a stroke and major head injury after a car accident that also resulted in the death of my wife. I am writing this because it is helping me to develop an adequate level to supernatural, psychological and physiological adjustments. It may help you as well. It has brought me security.

—*John F. Gillette, D.Min.*

Discovering
GOD'S
Heart

Feeling God's Heart Pulse

is Our Daily Challenge

JOHN F. GILLETTE
WITH JOY E. GILLETTE

Author of Discovering God's Favor and Discovering God's Presence

Chapbook Press
Schuler Books
2660 28th Street SE
Grand Rapids MI 49512

www.schulerbooks.com/chapbook-press

Discovering God's Heart: Feeling God's Heart Pulse is Our Daily Challenge

Copyright ©2016 — John F. Gillette. All rights reserved. Published 2016. Printed at Schuler Books, Chapbook Press, Grand Rapids, Michigan, in the United States of America.

First Edition 2016

Excerpts taken from Discovering God's Presence: A Pastoral Health Care Devotional, © 2015 by Dr. John F. Gillette, DSM, D.Min.

Distribution contact:at jjgillette@comcast.net.

ISBN 13: 9781948237130

Library of Congress Control Number: 2018964958

Cover photo: Greg Rakozy/Unsplash
Cover Design: Frank Gutbrod Graphic Design

Printed in the United States of America

The Pastoral Health Care Discovery Series was produced to help during difficult trials in life. It was developed through five volumes.

Adjustments are shared through God's sufficiency. It provides a basic spiritual solution strategy. We have to affirm, accept and adjust to God's plan of action. His superiority, sovereignty and sufficiency will bring victory.

Empowerment is given through God's love. The receiving of his Son Jesus Christ provides power. Historical facts declare the truth.

Enablement is given through God's counsel. Instruction, illumination and application provides the growing process in grace.

Encouragement is given through the awareness of God's kingdom. Learning to accept God's perspective is necessary. The Holy Spirit will travel with us in the present and the future.

Contentment is given through God's heart. The meditation model is the method to follow.

Table of Contents

Chapter 1
Meditation *01*

Chapter 2
Bible Authority *04*

Chapter 3
Bible Application *06*

Chapter 4
Bible Study *08*

Chapter 5
Preparing the Preparer *10*

Chapter 6
God's People Prepare for Christ's Birth *12*

Chapter 7
Cradle, Cross and the Crown *15*

Chapter 8
Christ is Always the Same *17*

Chapter 9
Adequate in Christ *19*

Chapter 10
Christ's Return *21*

Chapter 11
Church Attendance *23*

Chapter 12
True Worshiper *26*

Chapter 13
The Silent Testimony *28*

Chapter 14
The Dynamic Church *30*

Chapter 15
The Devoted Church *32*

Chapter 16
Code of Conduct *34*

Chapter 17
Life in Jesus' Style *37*

Chapter 18
The Umpire for Life *39*

Chapter 19
Fear *41*

Chapter 20
The Greatest of These *43*

Chapter 21
Christian Withdrawal *45*

Chapter 22
The Spiritual Christian *47*

Chapter 23
Spiritual Conflict *49*

Chapter 24
Believer's Obligation *51*

Chapter 25
The Unreachable *53*

Chapter 26
Empty Handed *55*

Chapter 27
Backward Solders *57*

Chapter 28
Spiritual Battles *59*

Chapter 29
Power in Our Lives *62*

Chapter 30
A Transforming Truth *64*

Chapter 31
Follow Me *66*

Chapter 32
That Blessed Hope *68*

Chapter 33
Praise the Lord *70*

Meditation

The Bible says, "Speak to yourselves in psalms, and hymns, and spiritual songs, singing and making melody in your hearts to the Lord" (Eph. 5:19). In the Christian life, the Psalms should always be a special blessing. Psalms 1 has been my favorite. I have gone to the first three verses of this Psalms many times. "Blessed is the man that walkest not in the counsel of the ungodly, nor standeth in the way of sinners, not sitteth in the seat of the scornful; but his delight is in the law of the Lord; and him his law doth he meditates day and night. And he shall be like a tree planted by the rivers of water that bringeth forth his fruit in his season; his leaf also shall not wither; and whatsoever he doeth shall prosper" (Psalm 1:1-3).

From these verses we see the importance of the believer's meditating on the Scriptures. The Amplified Bible renders verse two; "But his delight and desire are in the law of the Lord and on His law – the precepts, the instructions, and teachings of God". We are to think on the Scriptures during the day and even the night time when we are awake.

When we do this, we will be fruitful and grow to maturity like a tree planted by water. The Bible says, "Every scripture is God-breathed given by His inspirations and profitable for instruction, for reproof, and condition of sin, for correction of error and discipline in obedience, and for training in righteousness.

This is what the Word of God is and does. No believer can live an effective spiritual life without it. It was Jesus who said, "It is the spirit that quickeneth; the flesh profiteth nothing. The worlds hat I speak unto you, they are the spirit and the life" (John 6:63). Because the Word of God is so important to our spiritual lives, our spiritual effectiveness depends on our maintaining a daily time of mediating on the Scriptures. Let us center our thoughts on the Word of God. The results will be simply a reproduction of the Bible in our lives.

Bible Authority

The Bible says, "And he reasoned in the synagogue... and persuaded the Jews and Greeks... and he continued teaching the word of God among them" (Acts 18:4, 11). I know of no other way to give the authority of the Scriptures then to continue teaching the word. I would like to reason and persuade you but the Scripture is a living, vital agency with supernatural power in itself. Read the promise. "For as the rain cometh down and the snow from heaven, and returneth not thither, but watereth the earth, and maketh it bring forth and bud, that it may give seed to the sower, and bread to the eater: so shall my word be that goeth forth out of my mouth; it shall not return unto me void, but it shall accomplish that which I please, and it shall prosper in the thing whereto I sent it" (Isaiah 55:10, 11). To the same purpose Jeremiah has written: "Is not your word like as a fire? Saith the Lord; and like a hammer that breaketh the rock in pieces?" (Jeremiah 23:29. God uses His wording — "For the word of God is quick (living), and powerful (active) and sharper than any two-edged sword, piercing even to the dividing asunder of soul and spirit, and of the joints and marrow and is a discerner of the thoughts and intents (ideas) of the heart" (Hebrews 4:12).

The Bible is an ancient book for modern times. It is one book, one history, one story and one mind produced it. God Himself became a man so that we might know what to think of when we think of God (John 1:14, 14:9). I could give all the evidences for scriptural authority but why don't you read the Bible for yourself and let it prove itself.

Bible Application

The Bible says, "As newborn babes, desire the sincere milk of the word that ye may grow thereby" (I Peter 2:2). God has given his word so that believers may grow thereby. We haven't fulfilled our obligations to the word until application has taken place. The Bible is not only the source book for information but has life changing power for today. Growth in the spiritual life comes not merely from hearing but from hearing and doing. The Bible says, "the effectual doer shall be blessed in what he does" (James 1:25). If you know these things, you are blessed if ye do them (John 12:17).

The Bible has been given so that man's basic nature can be changed. "All Scripture is given by God and is profitable for teaching, for reproof, for correction, for training in righteousness, that the man of God may be adequate, equipped for every good work," (II Timothy 3:16, 17). It teaches, rebukes, restores trains for righteous living. It equips us to do the work that God wants us to do. The Bible convicts, regenerates, nurtures, cleanses, counsels, guides, prevents sin, revives, strengthens, gives wisdom, delivers, and helps. The Bible alone realistically and sufficiently meets man's deepest problems, longings, needs, and inadequacies. It provides the answers to man's needs for deliverance from the penalty of sin, for spiritual progress, daily victory, for guidance and personal relationships, and conduct. As we learn the Scriptures, let us apply it to our daily activities.

Bible Study

The Bible says, "Blessed are the undefiled in the way, who walk in the law of the Lord" (Psalm 119:1). What is wrong with reading the Bible? Why do people think it is so strange? Some people have the idea that the Bible is just for the mentally weak, some people think it is for the ignorant, some people imagine that it is only for the shut-ins, and some think that it is only for the children. Why do the teens, young adults turn from it? I believe they do not go on to read it or believe it or study it or follow it. If we are going to walk in the law of the Lord, we must follow this pattern.

First, we need to study it through. That is master a verse every day. Think of it, at the end of the year, you will have 365 verses in your heart and in our mind to bring about happiness, direction, peace, and contentment. We need to pray about it. We must let each verse become a part of our very being, praying the verse right into reality, and then seeing the promises of God as we claim them to change our lives. We must write down our thoughts. We cannot remember everything but our computer mind has it and we need to refresh our memory. That, of course, brings us to working it out. Let the Bible get in our heart and then live it out every day. It is not good only to study it through or pray about it or put it down or work it out, but we must also pass it on. We must talk about it. Let the Word of God inspire and bless your heart. It takes discipline. You cannot be lazy. Walk in the Law of the Lord and you will find purpose and peace.

Preparing the Preparer

The Bible says, "There was a man sent from God whose name was John. The same came for a witness to bear witness of the Light that all men through Him might believe" (John 1:6,7). Most people call Jesus' cousin "John the Baptist". That's not a bad name, but is it the best? Maybe he ought to be called something else, like "John the Preparer", for that was his most important purpose in life. God sent him to prepare the people for Jesus' coming. John told them: "Get ready, for the Lamb of God, who will take the sins of the word, is coming". Reading about John in the Bible, we see that he faithfully fulfilled this purpose in life. He preached repentance and preparation, getting the people ready for the appearance of Christ. John the Baptist can most certainly be called John the Preparer.

When we think about John, it is easy to forget something that is very important. We tend to forget that God was the one who actually made the preparation. He prepared the preparer. It was God who first of all determined that it was time for the preparer. He sent an angel to John's parents, Zacharias and Elizabeth, telling them that they would have as son. He told them what to name him. John grew up strong and sturdy in the body and spirit. In Luke 3:2 we are told that God spoke to John while he was living in the wilderness. God told him it was time to begin his great work. John obeyed God and in so doing fulfilled a great prophecy given by Isaiah many years before: "The voice of him that crieth in the wilderness; Prepare ye the way of the Lord". John prepared the way for Christ; but it was God who first prepared John. Behind all of John's preparation was God!

God's People Prepare for Christ's Birth

The Bible says, "I bring you the most joyful news ever announced. The Savior, the Messiah, The Lord has been born tonight in Bethlehem!" (Luke 2:10, 11).

Since the early days of the church, God's people have prepared for a proper celebration of Christmas. During this season Christians get ready on every level of life for a God-pleasing remembrance of celebration of the great day on which the Savior was born. It was a great day. On it for a moment God tore open the heavens and let the angelic ecstasy come down on the ears of men. It was the day that marked the beginning of the end for Satan and his power, and set the light of the world firmly in the midst of sin's inky blackness. It was a day eagerly anticipated by the prophets of old and joyfully remembered by His people of the New Age.

The evangelist John, frequently talked about Christ as the Light of the World. This name was not new to him. Isaiah, many years before, looking ahead to our world said, "The people that walked in darkness have seen a great light."

Christmas is all about this Light of the world. We know that there is still much darkness. It is a darkness made up of sin, ignorance, hate, and pride.

To remind themselves of the growing power of Christ, the Light, Christians have long made preparation for the celebration of Jesus' birth! We can say in a sense that we prepare for the coming of God. But the reverse is also true. God prepared for the coming of man. We are now on the very edge of Christmas. Even now God is speaking to us, saying; "if you haven't prepared before, prepare now! In my Son I will give you all that you need — peace, hope, happiness, and joy, when you accept Jesus as your Savior."

Prayer: Dear Lord, as we stand here face to face with Christmas, lead us to give our hearts to you. In Christ Jesus wipe away our sins of selfishness, pride and ingratitude. Make this Christmas a true spiritual experience that we may rejoice in you and your gift. Amen.

Cradle, Cross and the Crown

The Bible says, "God so loved the world that He gave His only begotten Son that whoever believeth in him should not perish but have everlasting life" (John 3:16). God loved the world so much He put His Son in the manger for a cradle, His Son on a cross for us and He gave Christ a crown.

God sent a baby to be born, not in the palace of a king, but in a lowly stable. Christ was born to a virgin and His cradle was a manger. That is why the Nativity Scene is a sacred reminder of the real reason for Christmas. It is so much more than parties, Santa Claus, the blaring of carols over loud speakers and all our frantic shopping.

Over that rough-hewn manger was the shadow of a cross. Christ went all the way to the cross to pay for our sins and reconcile us to God, and to tell us of God's great love.

Jesus, as King reigns over an eternal kingdom. It will continue when all earth's monarchies and dynasties have faded into oblivion. In Revelation 14:14, Christ is portrayed as having a golden crown.

In our traveling on the Christian way, we must not leave Christ in the manger. Christ went on to live a wonderful lie and gave His life on a cross and rose from the dead. We must have faith in the Christ of the cross.

We must also have a Crown faith that will claim Christ as sovereign.

We need all three symbols of our faith. The Cradle, the Cross and the Crown.

Christ is Always the Same

The Bible says, "Jesus Christ is the same yesterday, today and forever" (Hebrews 13:8). We must cherish our yesterdays, dream of tomorrow and live in today.

In our yesterdays many of us met Christ and accepted Him as Savior and Lord of our lives. We learned to trust Him ad obey Him. We found his love can daily lead us through depression, anxiety, pain, uncertainty, hardship and fears. We experienced the ability to face anything because He is always with us. Jesus' love never fails.

There comes time to dream of tomorrow. Plan for it. Seek God's guidance, "Trust in the Lord with all your heart, lean not unto thy own understanding. In all your ways acknowledge

Him and He will direct your path" (Prov. 3:5,6). Set long term and short-term goals for your life.

Live for today. Follow the Lord's directions and seek to accomplish the goals you have set under God's guidance and ask for His leadership and strength Live one day at a time. We must cherish our yesterdays, dream of tomorrow, and live life to its fullest today.

Adequate in Christ

The Bible says "who is the image of the invisible God, the firstborn of every creature" (Col 1:15). It is important for men to think. It is one of the facts of the human mind that a man only thinks as much as he has to. We must use the heart and mind that a man only thinks as much as he has to. We must use the heart and mind on this test. The 'who' in the verse is Christ. The word image is found in Hebrews 1:3. It says, "Who being the brightness of his glory, and the express image of his person. . . ." Christ is the reflection of God. He is the exact resemblance of God. He is the manifestation of God in the flesh.

The human soul is dark respecting the divine character until is enlightened by Christ. "Everything has been entrusted to me by my

Father. Only the Father knows the Son, and the Father is known only by the Son and by those to whom the Son reveals him. Come to me and I will give you rest". (Matthew 11:27-28). Christ is adequate to meet all our needs because He is God.

Christ's Return

The Bible says, "Ye men of Galilee, why stand ye gazing up into heaven, this same Jesus which is taken up from you into heaven, shall come in like manner as ye have seen Him go into heaven". (Acts 1:11)

His disciples expected Christ to return at any moment. In fact, the whole New Testament church held the perpetual hope of Christ's imminent return. The coming of Jesus demands that our lives count for Him. The Bible says in Revelation 22:6-7, "and he said unto me, these sayings are faithful and true and the Lord God of the Holy Prophets sent His angel to show unto His servants the things which must shortly be done... behold I come quickly, blessed is he that keepeth the sayings of the prophecy of this book".

Now notice in verse 6 the word, shortly. Means speedily. The promise is not that these events will happen soon, rather when they start, they will happen quickly. In verse 7, we see the words, I come quickly! The emphasis is once again placed on the true meaning of the text. When it comes, it is going to come fast and we must be alert to what is going to happen. The way to be alert and be prepared is by emphasizing the next word. He says, blessed is he that keepeth the sayings. Now what he is simply saying is that we are to observe his teachings. We are to be obedient to that teaching as we receive his revelation, which is the Bible, as we reflect upon it, as we research it, as we recite it, we will be prepared. Revelation isn't entertainment, it is motivation. We should sense the urgency of the hour, the seriousness of rejecting Jesus Christ, and then we must look at the blessedness of service that is ours until He does return.

Church Attendance

The Bible says, "Let us hold fast the profession of our faith without wavering for he is faithful that promised, and let us consider one another to provoke unto love and to good works, not forsaking the assembling of ourselves together as a matter of some is, but exhorting one another and so much the more as ye see the day approaching" (Hebrews 10:23-25).

I have been asked the question, "Why go to church?" There are many reasons why we should go to church because we are in an organic union with its head, because we have kinship relationship with its members, because the organized church is recognized in the New Testament, because the church is a self-developing body, because of the new resurrection fellowship day, because we are one in accord in witnessing, because we are to give of our tithes and gifts in obedience, because we are to keep God's memorial supper, because it is our duty. The duty, the command to gather is found in this text, "not forsaking the assembly". We find the same emphasis in II Thessalonians 2:1, "Now we beseech you brethren by the coming of our Lord Jesus Christ and by our gathering together unto him." There is no place for isolation regarding the believer. He is called to come together. We find in the text . . ." as the manner of some is . . ." this would imply that there are some that are neglecting it because of persecution, perhaps through fear, perhaps through the lack of interest, perhaps through doubting of its necessity, perhaps through dissatisfaction, and yet, the Bible says it is our sacred duty to gather together to exhort, which means to encourage or to admonish or to urge. For the day is approaching that Christ will return. Shouldn't we find ourselves together responding in obedience to His will? "There are two ways of stopping a clock; you can smash it or you can let it run down, and there are two ways of doing away with churches; you can destroy them or you can ignore them. If we are going to fight for the liberty of worship, we ought to make some use of that liberty.

True Worshiper

The Bible says, "But an hour is coming, and now is, when the true worshipers shall worship the Father in spirit and truth; for such people the Father seeks to be His worshipers" (John 4:23). What has happened to true worshipers today? Have we shaped our concepts of God to fit our own understanding? We have measured Him by our intellect and felt quite free to expect Him to answer all of our "why's" as though our brains were adequate to handle His answers. Have we worshiped only when we decided God had lived up to our expectations? God says, "For as the heavens are higher than the earth, so are My ways higher than your ways, and My thoughts than your thoughts" (Isaiah 55:9).

Worship involved three basic activities. The Bible says, "Come, let us worship and bow down" (Psalm 95:6). No worship takes place without humbling ourselves. Paul's greatest chapter on humility is Philippians 2, and his greatest chapter on worship is Philippians 3. The one leads to the other. Kneeling goes against the grain of every prideful bone in us but it helps.

Worship involves casting our crowns before the throne (Revelation 4:10). A "Crown" is anything that exalts the wearer. If it draws attention to the person wearing it, then it's a crown. No man who worships Jesus Christ ever wants to be exalted. He is too involved with Christ to demand notice of his own crowns.

The third activity of a worshiper of Jesus Christ is telling the Lord His worth-ship. The Bible says, "Worthy art thou, our Lord and our God, to receive glory and honor and power" (Revelation 4:11). Get alone often to tell the Lord what He is worth to you. Worship is mandatory. In fact, it's the only essential activity on earth.

The Silent Testimony

The Bible says, "And all the multitudes kept silent and gave audience to Barnabas and Paul declaring what miracles and wonders God had wrought among the Gentiles by them" (Acts 15:12).

I believe this is descriptive of the 20th Century Christianity. I must ask the question of why do the Christians fail to vocalize their testimony? Several reasons have come to mind. Possibly one is that they lack genuine conviction. They do not really comprehend the important facts that Jesus Christ is the only way to God, that eternal condemnation waits for all who reject Him. When we truly acknowledge our sinfulness and our inability to save ourselves and place our trust in Christ, God forgives us and receives us into His family and there is a genuine positive testimony because of the conviction we have in Christ Jesus.

We do not vocalize our testimony because of the lack of spiritual courage. The Bible says, "whosoever therefore shall be ashamed of me at my words in this adulterous and sinful generation, then also shall the Son of Man be ashamed, when He cometh in the glory of His Father with the Holy Angels" (Mark 8:38). We do not want to be labeled as a spiritual fanatic. We do not want to be ridiculed or have our sensitivity hurt. We may be embarrassed about ourselves and the quality of our service for Christ, but we never need to be ashamed of our Savior or be afraid to declare that we are His followers. I think we have no excuse. Once we become grounded with the Word of God, it will penetrate our heart, it will melt our resistance, and it will silence any argument that we may come up with to be silent for the testimony that Christ lives in us.

The Dynamic Church

The Bible says, "So we, being many, are one body in Christ, and every one member's one of another" (Romans 12:5).

Often as you read through the New Testament, you will see the two words, one another. In this verse, we find that the word "many" of course means numerous and that there are many individuals that make up the church, or the body of Christ. The body of Christ is the uniting of individuals that have put Jesus Christ first in their lives. They are in union with Christ. We see the words, "in Christ". This is a brief preposition meaning that we are joined to Him in union. He is our head, He is our lawgiver, He is our counselor, He is our guide, and He is our Redeemer! Then the verse says, members of 'one another'. What a beautiful picture this is. We are a part of one another. Paul often illustrates this by the physical. The body has eyes, arms, a heart, legs and feet. But they are all a part of one body. Each person that has accepted Christ first in their life is a part of the body. They are members of 'one another'. Can you imagine what would happen in the church today if each member would realize this truth? We are a part of 'one another', so we are sensitive to each other's needs. We are interested in 'one another'. It is like the husband and wife relationship . . . caring and loving. And yet, we look at the church and we find so often individuals that are playing a part of an individual when they need to realize that they are a part of the whole. Each one is very important.

The Bible say, "But now they are many members, yet one body and the eye cannot say to the hand, I have no need of you nor again the head to the feet, I have no need of you" (I Corinthians 12:20,21). Let us function as the church should by realizing we are members of 'one another'.

The Devoted Church

The Bible says, "So we, being many, are one body in Christ, and every one member's one of another" (Romans 12:5). With this verse, we need to include another. It says "be kindly affectionate to one another with brotherly love, honoring and giving preference to one another."

When we read these words "kindly affectionate", they are nowhere else in the New Testament and it means 'tender'. In other words, when we are one another in Christ, we are to have this tender affection for one another. We are able to have that because of what Christ is doing in our lives, because we have something in common, because we believe in the same principles, and have the same interest. God tells us in John 13:34-35, "a new commandment I give unto you that you love one another as I have loved you, that ye also love one another, by this all will know that you are my disciples if ye have love for one another." The badge of the believer is brotherly love. But perhaps we are not able to love until some other things are taken care of. Maybe it is necessary for us to be patient with one another with so many different personalities, maybe some different peculiarities, so patience is necessary. Perhaps it is necessary for us to love ourselves before we can love others. God will help us do this loving for it is a sign of His presence within us.

The verse continues with the thought of honoring and giving preference to others. This simply means that we are to show or manifest respect for one another. If it is done, it will promote happiness, it will produce contentment, it will bring about harmony, therefore, to be a devoted church is one that is in love with one another.

Code of Conduct

The Bible says, "Obey God with deep reverence for God is at work in you, helping you want to obey Him and then helping you do what He wants" (Phil. 2:12,13). Obey God and you "will behave thyself wisely in a perfect way" (Psalm 101:2). Examine this code of conduct and you will find what is right or wrong for you to do in your life.

CONVERSION — turning to God from sin, "Thus it is written and thus it behooved Christ to suffer, and to rise from the dead the third day; and that repentance and remission of sins should be preached in His name" (Luke 24:46, 47), the necessity of becoming a member of God's family through accepting, trusting, and believing in Jesus Christ.

CONSECRATION — dedication to God, "I beseech you therefore, brethren" (Romans 12:1,2) the necessity of having Jesus Christ as Lord of your life "that ye might prove what is the perfect will of God".

CONSCIENCE — inner judge of moral issues, "Their conscience also bearing witness and their thoughts I have lived in all good conscience before God" (Romans 2:15). The necessity of having a good and pure conscience to give witness of right and wrong, not a conscience that is evil, defiled or seared.

COMMON SENSE OR RIGHTEOUSNESS — "If ye know that he is righteous, ye know that everyone that doeth righteousness is born of Him" (I John 2:29). The necessity of acknowledging Christ by our lives. Others watch us to see if we "do righteousness". He who abides in Christ will bear the same fruit in his life that Christ bore.

COMMISSION — special assignment given is "Go ye therefore and observe all things whatsoever I have commanded you; and, lo, I am with you always even unto the end of the world," (Matthew 28:19, 20) the necessity of becoming active in His work, the church. The Bible says, "Hold to ad offer to all men the Word of Life" (Phil. 2:16a). This is the secret to true success in life.

Life in Jesus' Style

The Bible says, "As you therefore have received Christ the Lord so walk in Him" (Colossians 3:6). I am concerned with walking in Him. How do I walk in Him? After receiving Jesus Christ as Savior, He must then become our Lord. We are to obey His commands. There is a sense of urgency in the command. This is a spiritual wardrobe. Our lifestyle is the manner in which we relate to others, spend our time, and express our individuality. We must communicate the characteristics that Christ communicated in His day. The first one is found in the word mercy. Compassion is drawn from that word. It really means to live in another's skin and to feel what he feels and to sense what he is going through. Today, we need to have this Christ-like compassion. The challenge is to let Christ reach out through us to others in the way He did to people in His earthly ministry.

The Umpire for Life

The Bible says, "Let the peace of God rule in your heart" (Col. 3:15). Another translation for that text is "let the ruling principles in your hearts be Christ's peace." For a person to follow this rule, they must have received Christ according to John 1:12. The peace of God refers to allowing peace to be the ruling force, principle or umpire in your life.

We must ask these questions and honestly answer them in regard to all of our daily activities if we are going to practice this truth: Is it in keeping with His Word? Would Jesus do it? Will it bring us closer to Him and each other?

Perfect peace cannot be purchased. It is our possession by trusting God through Christ completely. "Thou wilt keep him in perfect peace whose mind is stayed on thee; because he trusteth in thee. Trust ye in the Lord forever; for in the Lord Jehovah is everlasting strength" (Isaiah 26:3).

If we follow His plan and purpose, which is found in the Scriptures, we will have peace with God and the peace of God.

Fear

The Bible says, "Blessed is every one that fears the Lord" (Psalm 128:1). Fear is two-fold. It represents awe, reverence, especially toward God as the supreme. The results should be trust and confidence. When we fear God, we do not cringe before Him but a satisfying peace comes over us. "Be not afraid" (Proverbs 3:25, 26). "My God shall supply all your needs" (Phil. 4:19).

It also represents a painful emotion marked by dread and anxious concern. The Bible says, "Never be troubled about tomorrow, for tomorrow will take care of itself. The days' own trouble is enough for the day" (Matthew 6:34). God gives us manageable portions one day at a time. Suppose all the future was given to us at one time, we would be overwhelmed. God broke life up into small portions which we can manage one day at a time. So, forget the yesterdays, do not try to face tomorrow, deal with today. Life by the yard is hard. Life by an inch is a cinch.

You ask what do I do about the yesterdays and the tomorrows? If you belong to God through Jesus Christ, He has all your yesterdays and forgives all that was amiss in them. He will give grace and power to face your anxieties for tomorrow. He will not provide for what is not here. He will help only as they come. His grace is like manna, when kept over the next day, it spoiled. When fearful, be encouraged, the weight of all your fears and anxieties are upon God, but He takes them one day at a time.

The Greatest of These

The Bible says, "And now abideth Faith, Hope and Love, these three, but the great of these is Love" (I Cor. 13:13). The greatest of these words were written by the apostle Paul to the Corinthian Christians.

Corinth, the commercial metropolis of Greece, was one of the largest cities in the Roman Empire. The vices of the East and West met in this evil city, but here Paul founded one of his greatest churches. Three years later a delegation of the Corinthian Church came to Ephesus to consult Paul about some very serious problems.

At that time the Christians met in homes, or in halls, or wherever they could, thousands of Christians divided into small groups under their own leadership. They were developing into small rival units rather than cooperating units, in the cause of Christ.

In Paul's letter he deals with their many problems. He urges the Corinthian Christians to earnestly desire and cultivate the higher gifts, and choice graces. Yet, he says, "I will show you a more excellent way, one that is better by far and highest of them all — Love."

Paul says all special gifts and powers from God shall some day come to an end, but love remains. God's love in us is the perfection of human character, the most powerful force in the universe and the essence of God's nature. The church's most effective weapon.

Christian friend, may I urge you to eagerly pursue and seek to acquire this love. Make it your aim, your great quest. For faith, hope and love abide but the greatest of these is love. God's love in us; irresistible, undying, and eternal. The love of God is greater far than tongue or pen can ever tell.

Christian Withdrawal

The Bible says, "go therefore and make disciples of all the nations . . ." (Matthew 28:10). We need to hear Jesus' urgent call, "Get into the world." Too many of us hide from non-Christians, as if we were undercover agents. Someone has said, "We are like the Saint Lawrence Seaway-frozen at the mouth." As Christians, we should not isolate ourselves, but infiltrate the world. To be in the world is to feel the pain of our friends: to share the hurt of a friend who has divorced parents, to pat the back of a friend who was cut from the team, to sit next to the person who always sits alone. No matter who we are, we need to be able to be touched by the huts of our friends. To be in the world is to be emotionally, physically, mentally and socially involved.

It is amazing how much we have in common with all people. We are not to isolate ourselves. Worldliness is not an external thing. It is internal. Jesus never said, "Get out of the world," but He says, "Get the world out of you!" There is nothing wrong with having non-Christian friends. Jesus had all kinds of them. He gave a prediction, "In the last days, wickedness will be multiplied and most men's love will grow cold." (Matthew 24:12). If ever the followers of Jesus were called on to be different, it is today. If ever we need to learn how to say, "No compromise!" it is today. Jesus said, "I do not pray that thou should keep them safe from the evil one" (John 17:15). To say "No compromise!" is to say "I know God made me just the way I am. It is to say, "He is my leader. Therefore, don't withdraw yourself but dare to be different and get involved.

The Spiritual Christian

The Bible tells us that there are three kinds of men. One, the natural man; two, the carnal Christian man; and three, the spiritual Christian man. God's ideal is that we might become Spiritual Christians, those who walk by the spirit. Would you like a touch of Heaven here on earth? Well, there are certain conditions that we must meet. The result will be the filling of the spirit" (I Thess. 5:19). The first condition is to stop resisting the spirit, stop saying no to his guidance, stop refusing the yield to the Word of God as He brings it home to you. We find in this little verse that we should be in a constant attitude of yielding rather than rebellion. Remember, this is not only in connection with the seemingly major issues of God's plan for our life in the future, but it also applies to all of the multitude of incidents and decisions that make up each day.

"Quench not the spirit" means not to suppress the spirit. It has nothing to do with extinguishing the spirit or losing him once he indwells a believer. The problem is one of accepting and doing the will of God. The foundation of communion and fellowship are confession, yielding, and dependence.

Spiritual Conflict

The Bible says, "And grieve not the Holy Spirit of God" (Eph. 4:30). The second condition is stop sinning against the spirit We grieve the spirit when we go contrary to His Holy person. Our fellowship is with a person and this relationship can never be right as long as we continue in unconfessed and unforsaken sin, as the Carnal Christian has done. The Bible says, "If we say that we have not sin, we deceive ourselves, and truth is not in us" (I John 1:8). You see, all the believers have a sinful nature. All believers commit sinful acts. The Bible says, "If we say that we have not sinned, we make Him a liar, and His word is not in us" (I John 1:10). The Bible says that the believer who does not confess His sin is disciplined or corrected by God. The Holy Spirit should dominate the believer's total person. The presence of sin in the believer's total person. The presence of sin in the believer's life grieves the Holy Spirit. The Holy Spirit wants to minister through the Christian, not plead with him to repent. While on earth, we will always have conflict with our fallen nature. Sin is always sin in the sight of God. The cure is confession to God.

Believer's Obligation

The Bible says, "This I say then, walk in the spirit, and ye shall not fulfill the lust of the flesh" (Gal. 5:16). The third condition is then to stop walking in the flesh. This verse means a moment by moment or step by step relationship with the spirit who dwells within you. The carnal Christian is exhorted to walk by His person and His power. The Bible says, "As ye have therefore received Christ Jesus the Lord, so walk ye in Him" (Col. 2:6). It is the believer's obligation to maintain an attitude of confidence and expectation toward the Holy Spirit. We need to practice a conscious and habit-forming dependence upon His enabling power, Greater is he that is in you than he that is in the world" (I John 4:4).

The Bible says, "And be not drunk with wine . . . but be filled with the Spirit" (Eph. 5:18). This means, instead of being constantly under the domination of win, be dominated by the spirit of God constantly. We also find here that the spiritual experience is a moment by moment walk with the spirit not one grand experience which solves all the problems of the Christian life.

The Unreachable

"And Jesus said, if ye have faith as a grain of a mustard seed, nothing shall be impossible for you" (Matt. 17:20). The mustard seed is the smallest of all seeds, but it produces the largest of all herbs. Therefore, if you have an increasing, expanding, growing faith from the beginning, eventually you will be able to perform the most difficult undertakings. Jesus saith, "Have faith in God for verily I say unto you, that whosoever shall say unto this mountain be thou removed, and be thou cast into the sea; and shall not doubt him his heart, but shall believe those things which he saith shall come to pass; he shall have whatsoever he saith. Therefore, I say unto you, what things so ever ye desire, when ye pray, believe that ye receive them, and ye shall have them" (Mark 11:22-24).

As Christians, we have trusted, put our confidence in Jesus Christ, and believe that He is God. He died as a Savior for our sins. He rose from the dead to become the Lord of our lives. It has taken faith to believe; now we go a step further. As our relationship with God personally becomes reliant in character, "Nothing shall be impossible unto us." We do this by knowing God through attending His divinity school, letting the Holy Spirit teach us God's revealed truth. With increasing knowledge of God, our fellowship with Him advances. In understanding and applying this verse, our mustard seed of faith will expand to the unreachable.

Empty Handed

The Bible says, "And let the beauty of the Lord our God be upon us: and establish thou the work of our hands upon us; yea, the work of our hands establishes thou it" (Psalm 90:17). "Work with your hands, as we commanded you" (I Thess. 4:11). When we think about hands, we think of service. We think of working for our God. Here are some reasons why we might end up empty-handed.

Every Christian's responsibility is to be a witness for Jesus Christ. Are we obeying God's command? Go tell the story and make disciples and win people to Christ.

Every Christian's responsibility is to be soul-conscious not material conscious. Are we too busy making a living for ourselves to have compassion for a world without Christ?

Every Christian's responsibility is to bear fruit. God wants fruit, the kind of fruit that has those Christ-like qualities listed in Galatians 5 (Fruit of the Spirit). Are we producing fruit that will draw the un-Christian to Christ?

I believe when we get involved, God begins to do unusual and wonderful things. Let's have some trophies when we face the Savior at the judgement seat. The Apostle Paul said, "you Thessalonian Christians, I've won to the Lord you are my joy and crown of rejoicing at his coming" (I Thess. 2:19, 20). Paul said, "When I stand there, you are my trophies of grace. I can present to the Savior you precious souls I have led to Christ!" We do not want to slack in this matter. Must I go, and empty-handed? Must I meet my Savior so? Not one soul with which to greet Him must I empty-handed go.

Backward Soldiers

The Bible says, "Thou therefore, my son, be strong in the grace that is in Christ Jesus… endure hardness as a good soldier of Jesus Christ". The faith that guides the footsteps of so many finds its militant peak in the vibrant, stirring and faith stimulating "Onward Christian Soldiers".

We sing and play this song as the war with the cross of Jesus going on before but our souls seem to be born in jelly.

All that the world has to do with us is run us into molds and make us into any shape it chooses. We are soldiers that are going backward to defeat. Our ideas are made for us just as our clothes. Our external person should never be changed by mere fashion, it should have a voice in the world, its own voice, eve though it be the faintest whisper. Let us halt the backward movement and move forward to victory as good soldiers of Jesus Christ.

Spiritual Battles

The Bible says, "be of sober spirit, be on the alert, your adversary, the Devil, prowls about like a roaring lion seeking someone to devour" (I Peter 5:8). Christians today face many spiritual battles We must keep in mind that Satan is the one who ultimately desires that we pursue the lusts of the flesh, and it is he who sits as the god of this world (Eph. 2:1-10). Though not always directly involved, Satan's prime objective is the defeat of God and that means our defeat. The Bible says, "we have authority over the enemy, behold I give unto you power to tread on serpents and scorpions and over all the power of the enemy, and nothing shall by ant means hurt you". The world, power, there should be translated authority. It says, behold I give you authority over the power of the enemy. The Christian does not have power over Satan. He has authority over Satan.

When Jesus Christ was raised from the dead, we see the act of the resurrection and the surrounding events as one of the greatest workings of God manifested in the Scriptures. The Scripture says, "what is the surpassing greatness of his power toward us who believe. These are in accordance with the working of the strength of his might which he brought about in Christ when he raised him from the dead and seated him at his right hand in the heavenly places, far above all rule and authority and dominion and power, and every name that is named, not only in this age, but also in the one to come. He put all things in subjection under his feet and gave him his head over all things to the church which is his body. The fullness of him who fills all in all" (Eph. 1:19-23). Satan was defeated and disarmed. All of this unleashing of God's might and the resurrection, the ascension, and the seating of Jesus Christ was for you and me, that we might gain victory right now over sin. The source of our authority over Satan is rooted in God and His power.

Power in Our Lives

The Bible says, "Ye have not because ye ask not" (James 4:2-3). Praying is serious business. When you pray, you are talking to God. When you read the Bible, God is talking to you. I hear some people ask why do we have so little victory over sin? Or why do I have no answers to my prayers?

There is no reason why we can't experience power in our daily lives through prayer. It begins with believing what the Bible says. Let's search for God through Jesus Christ, he said, "I am the way, the truth and the life; no man cometh unto the Father, but by Me" (John 14:6). We must respond to the question in Acts 16:30, "What must I do to be saved?" and the answer is simply to believe in the Lord Jesus Christ and thou shalt be saved

(Acts 16:31). By Christ's sufferings and death, he solved the problems of personal sins and the problem of the sin nature. When a person believes in Christ, he participated in Christ's crucifixion, death, burial and resurrection (Romans 6:1-10). Since this has been accomplished, judgement against the sin nature and the victory over daily sin is possible. To put this into actual use, we must believe that I cannot measure up to God's standards on my own merits. I must receive God's remedy for sin and death. I must ask Jesus Christ to come into my heart. When we believe, power comes into our lives (John 1:12).

A Transforming Truth

The Bible says, "but God commandeth his love toward us in that, while we were yet sinners, Christ died for us" (Romans 5:8). It would be wonderful if everyone were living a joyous, victorious, love-filled life, but that is just not the case. All too many people are painfully aware of their weaknesses and shortcomings. As a result, they are thoroughly discouraged, having been overwhelmed by a sense of failure.

Because of this, ministers, counselors and psychologists are continually confronted with people who are downhearted because they cannot be what they know they ought to be. There is good news. You need not live in perpetual spiritual defeat God loves you. Out of all the billions of people who have ever lived. You are the object of the Lord's special concern. He has provided for your salvation, and you have every right to say with the apostle Paul, "I live by the faith of the son of God, who loved me and gave himself for me" (Galatians 22:20).

If you have ever felt discouraged or disheartened because you think you are not of much worth in God's sight, then I urge you to remember that you are the object of His redeeming love. As you accept the truth of God's love and apply it to your life, you will begin to experience happiness and your life will bring honor and glory to the Lord.

Follow Me

Jesus said, "He that followeth me shall have the Light of Life" (John 8:12). Follow me all along life's rugged pathway, through the valleys shadowed deep; overheated sands of deserts, up the mountains high and steep. Listen to the voice clear, vibrant compelling. God's voice was a composite of many harmonies. It was gentle with an all-encompassing love of authority and promise. In his voice was the omnipotent power of worlds in creation, the music of morning stars singing together, the gently murmur of a brook, the surety of a leader, and the certainty of a Master.

His voice echoes within the chambers of my heart. Its challenge rings in my ear. Have you caught a glimpse of the glory of service, of a glory that for a moment shone with wonderous brightness around, above and beyond the stranger who calls so simply, "follow me?" Of course, I will follow Him even to the end of the earth. Jesus calls, I must follow. My tomorrows are all known to thee and thou will lead me all the way.

Jesus of Nazareth is still passing by and still calling men to follow Him. The same voice is still speaking the same invitation. Will you hear Him? Will it be today or tomorrow or was it yesterday? Were you too busy with the pressures of life to heed?

That Blessed Hope

The Bible says, "He will come again in like manner as you have seen Him go" (Acts 1:1). This is he blessed hope. There is a two-fold purpose for Christ's coming again. First, to raise the dead in Christ. If this is true, how can we go on just living for earthly things with a hope like that in our soul? The Bible gives the plan of salvation and tells of Christ and the coming redemption from cover to cover. The dead in Christ are all those who died believing in Him; having accepted Him as their Savior and Lord.

The second reason for His coming again is to catch away all living believers; together with the raised dead. What could this mean? Who are the living believers? What do we have to do to the one? There is nothing for us to do, but has all been done for us by Christ. But, we must accept what Christ has done for us.

We have to believe that Christ came into the world to save sinners. He died on the cross to take our sins; yours, mine, and everyone so we can stand in God's presence clothes in Christ's righteousness.

There could be no greater heaven than to be caught-away with God's own, and spend eternity with Christ and our loved ones.

Praise the Lord

The Bible says, "Praise ye the Lord" (Psalm 146:1). The word "Hallelujah," occurs twenty-four times in the book of Psalms, and four times in in the nineteenth chapter of Revelation, making twenty-eight times altogether in the Bible. In the Psalms it is the Hallelujah of earth and in Revelations it is the Hallelujah of Heaven.

Let's look at the Hallelujah of Providence found in Psalm 105. It deals with the history of Israel and the psalmist sees the footprints of God in history as in nature. It was God who covenanted with Abraham "made an oath unto Isaac" and "confirmed the same to Jacob." It was God who protected His people when they were but few in number. It was God who called for a famine upon the land when prosperity had caused them to forget His laws. It was God who sent Joseph into Egypt, and then Moses as the deliverer of His people. It was God who sent the darkness and turned their water into blood. It was God who spread the clouds over them for a covering and gave them fire to give light in the night. It was God who opened the rock and quenched their thirst. The psalmist closes this review of God's providential dealings with a "Hallelujah".

More Books in the Series:

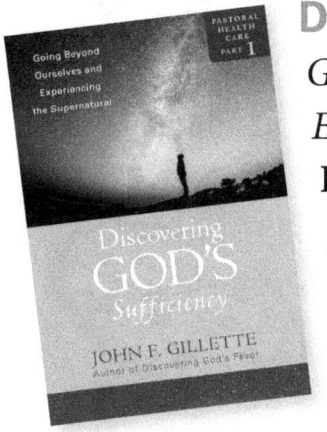

Discovering God's Sufficiency
Going Beyond Ourselves and Experiencing the Supernatural
Pastoral Health Care—Part One

Can anyone fix our troubles? The answer is 'yes.' How do we conquer our trials? We have to affirm God's intervention. We have to accept God's indwelling. We have to make some adjustments through God's illumination. We can experience God's power, presence and peace.

Discovering God's Love
Confirming God's love through the evidence of historical facts
Pastoral Health Care—Part Two

We can obtain strength to conquer through a knowledge of the 'Gospels' and receiving Jesus Christ into our hearts. The New Testament books of history give evidence of God's love. Through his love and faith, we are able to be strengthened, experience his support and become steadfast.

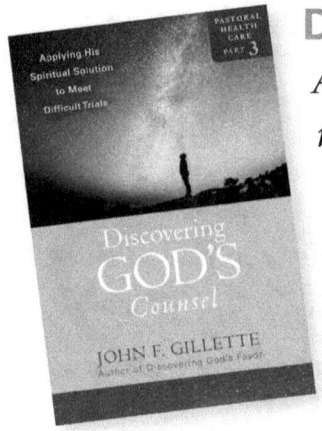

Discovering God's Counsel
Applying his spiritual solution to meet difficult trials
Pastoral Health Care—Part Three

Dark days can be life threatening. We have to develop an adequate level of spiritual, psychological and physiological adjustments. We can live with confidence in God's sufficiency.

Discovering God's Kingdom
Finding a way to understand ourselves in a complex world
Pastoral Health Care—Part Four

Dealing with life, death, heaven and eternity with God's perspective is necessary. It involves a personal decision of belief, trust and faith. Knowledge and commitment will bring comfort and security. The eternal destiny directive will provide the way.